LEARN SPANISH FOR KIDS SPANISH FOR CHILDREN (BODY PARTS)

Children's Foreign Language Learning Books

Speedy Publishing LLC
40 E. Main St. #1156
Newark, DE 19711
www.speedypublishing.com

The human body (cuerpo humano) includes the entire structure of a human being.

English
hair

Spanish
pelo

Hair is made mostly of a protein called keratin.

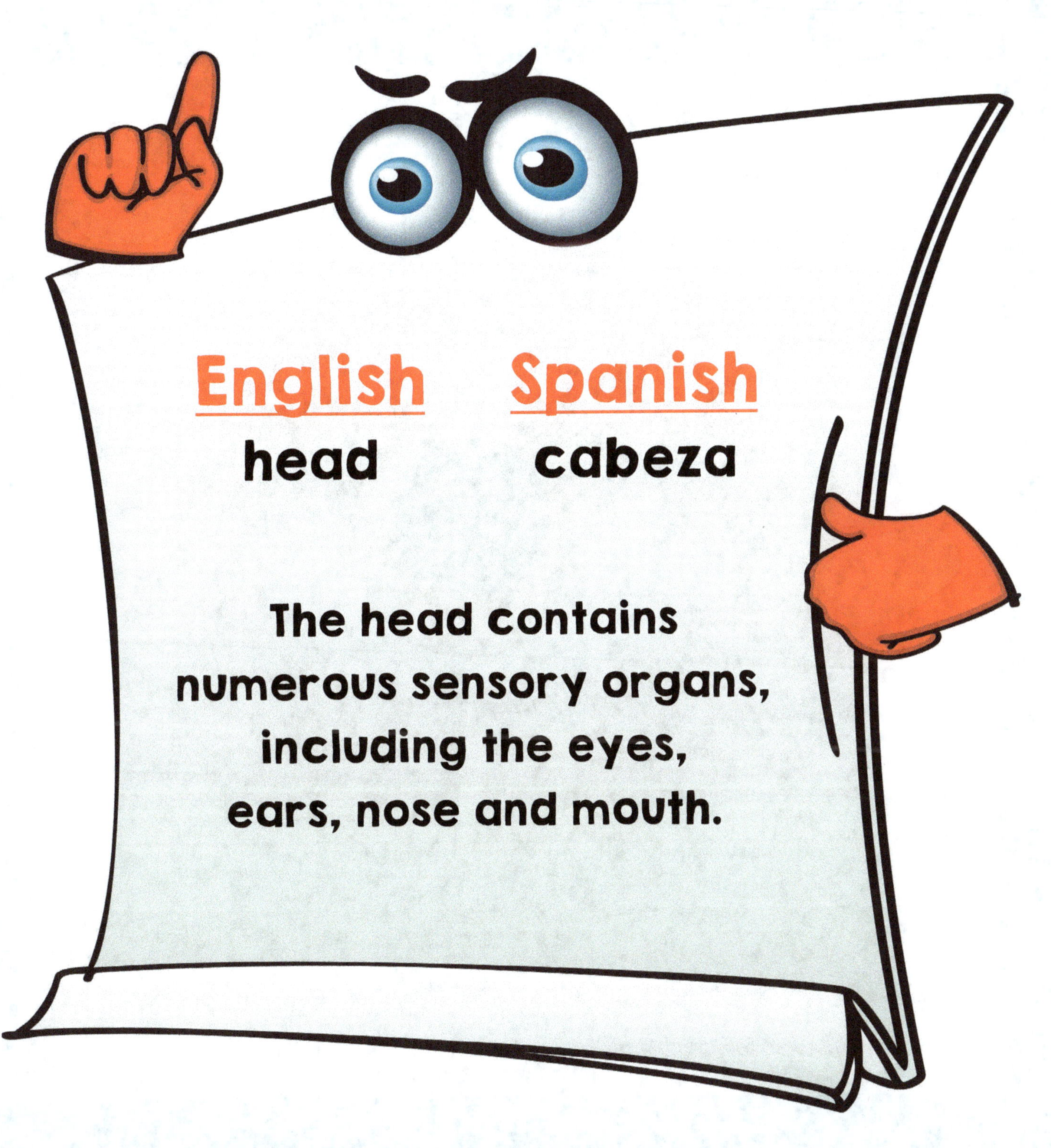

English
head

Spanish
cabeza

The head contains
numerous sensory organs,
including the eyes,
ears, nose and mouth.

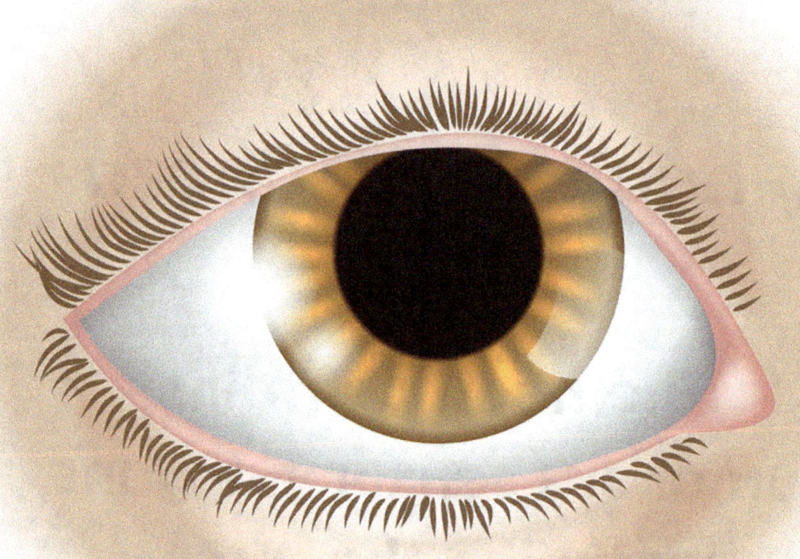

English
Spanish
eye
ojo
Your eyes are at work from the moment you wake up to the moment you close them to go to sleep.

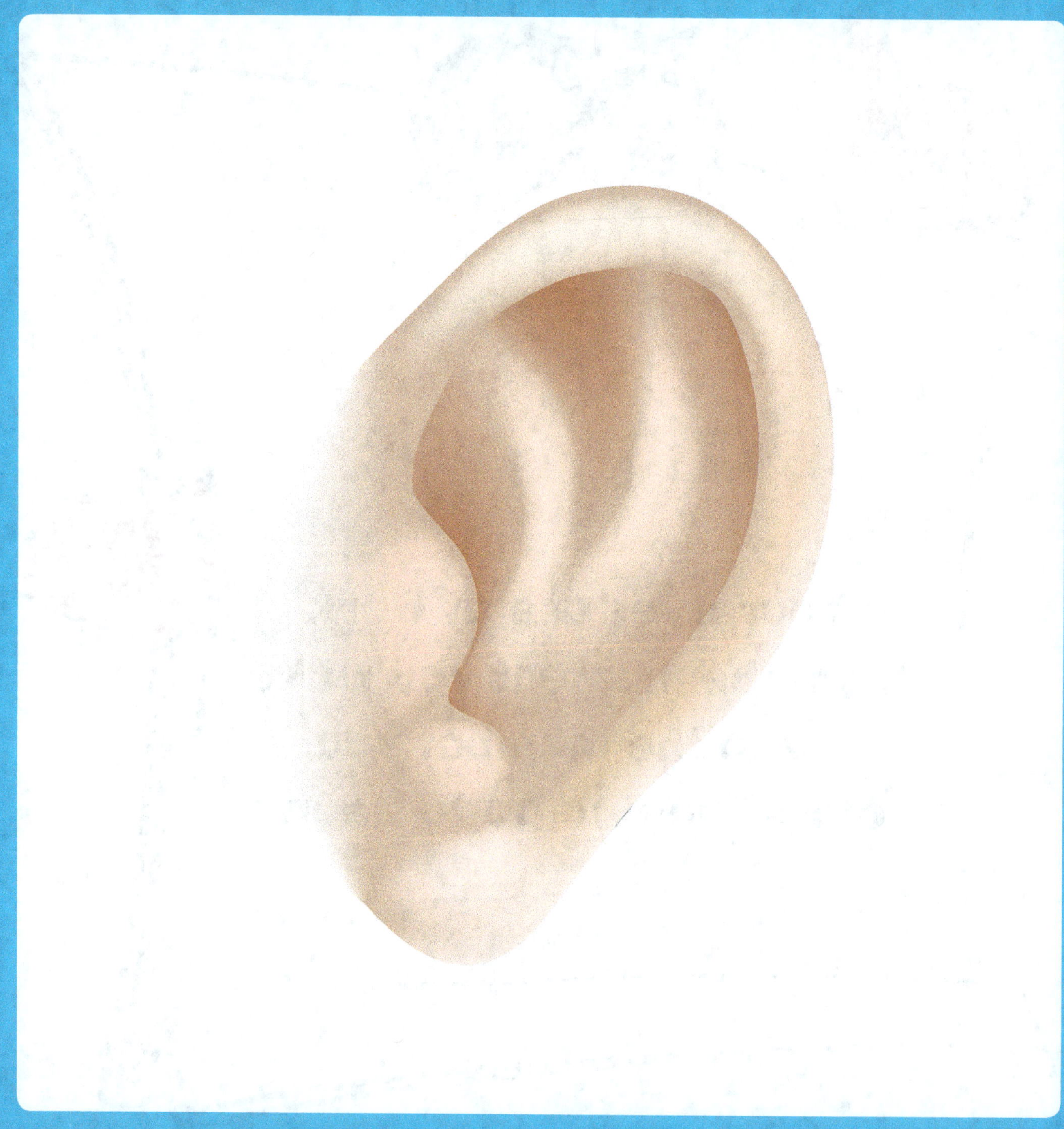

English
Spanish
ear
oreja
Our ears help us detect sound. Ears convert sound waves into nerve impulses that are sent to the brain.

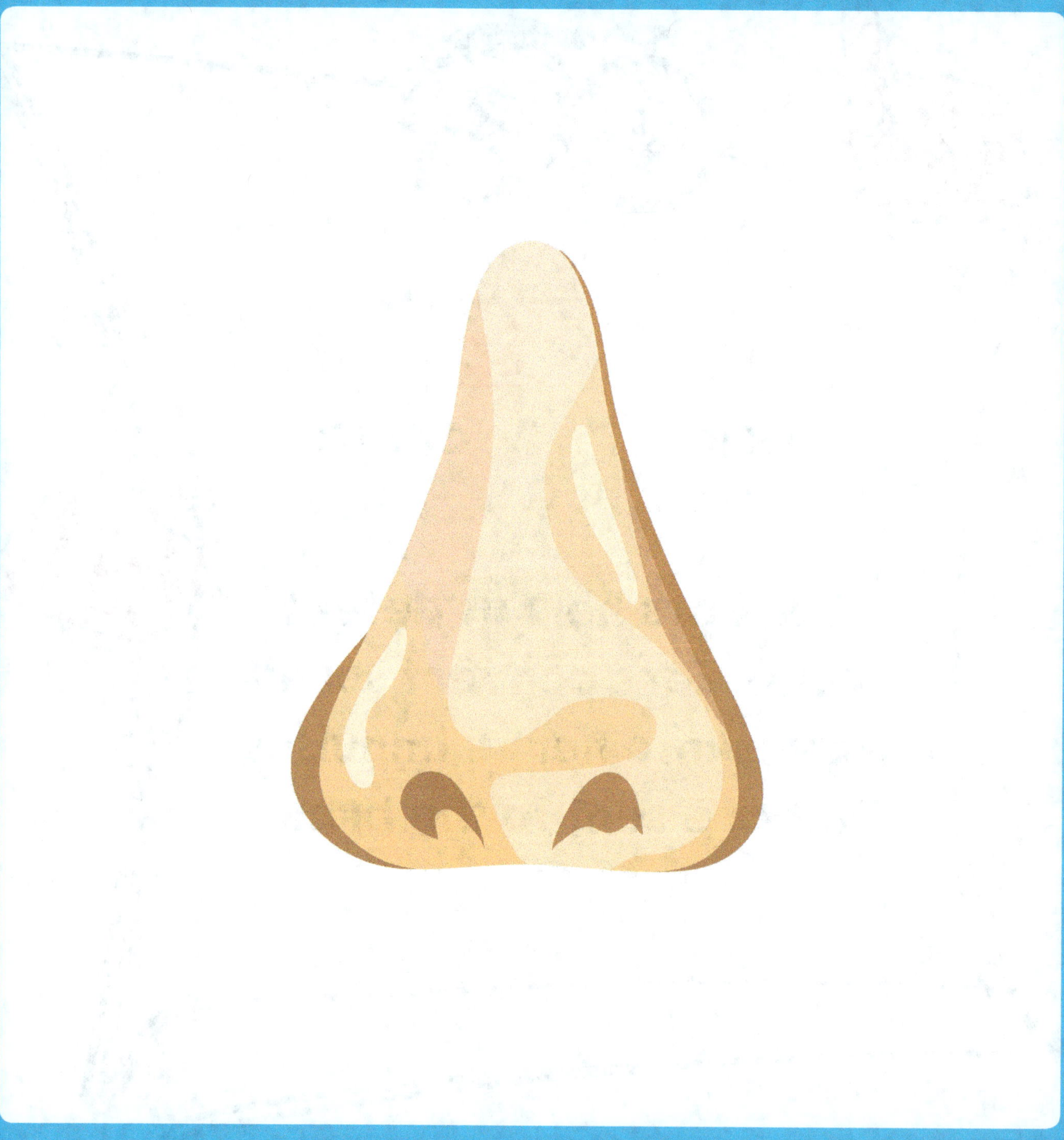

English
Spanish
nose
nariz
Your nose warms
air before it heads
to your lungs.

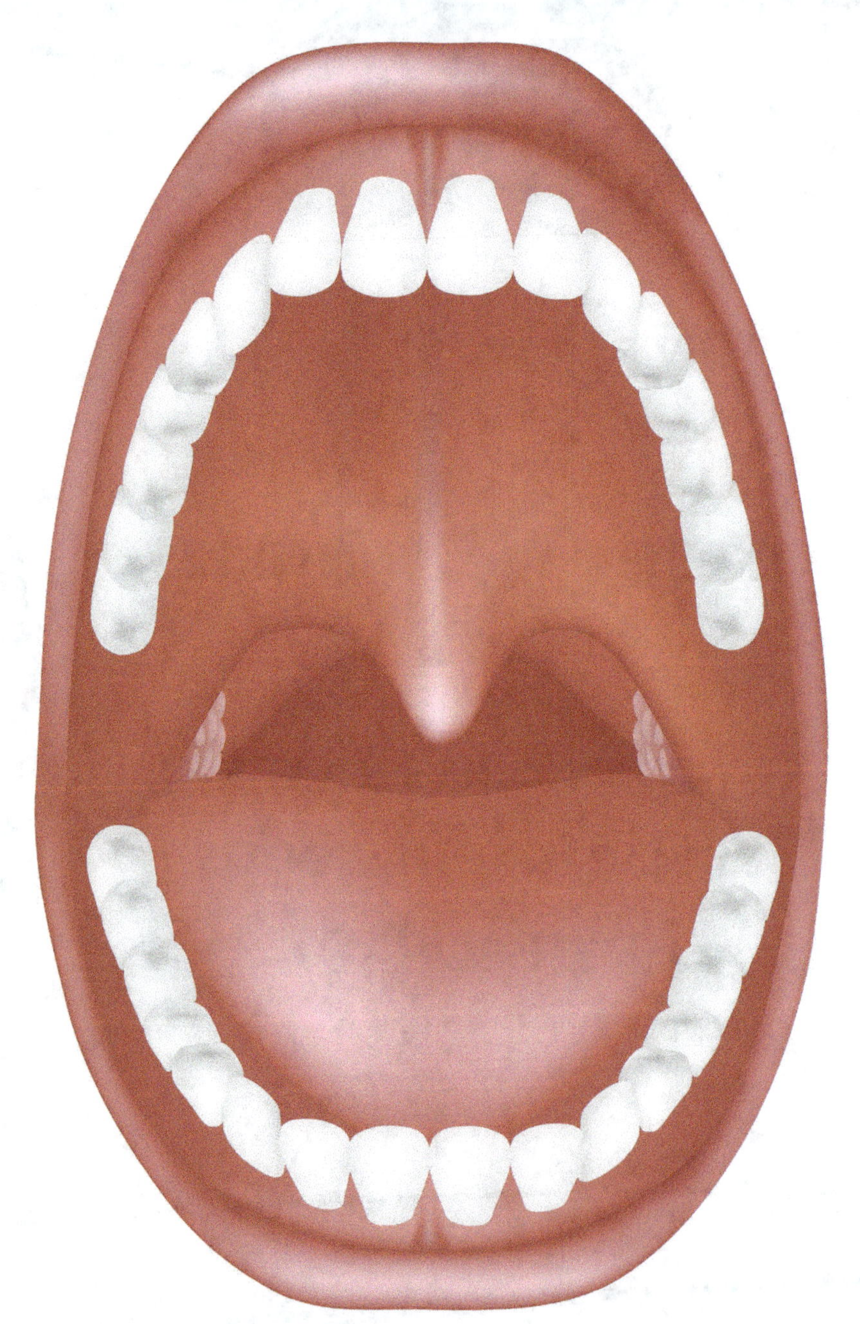

English
mouth

Spanish
boca

The mouth allows us
to talk, to smile or
frown, and to whistle.

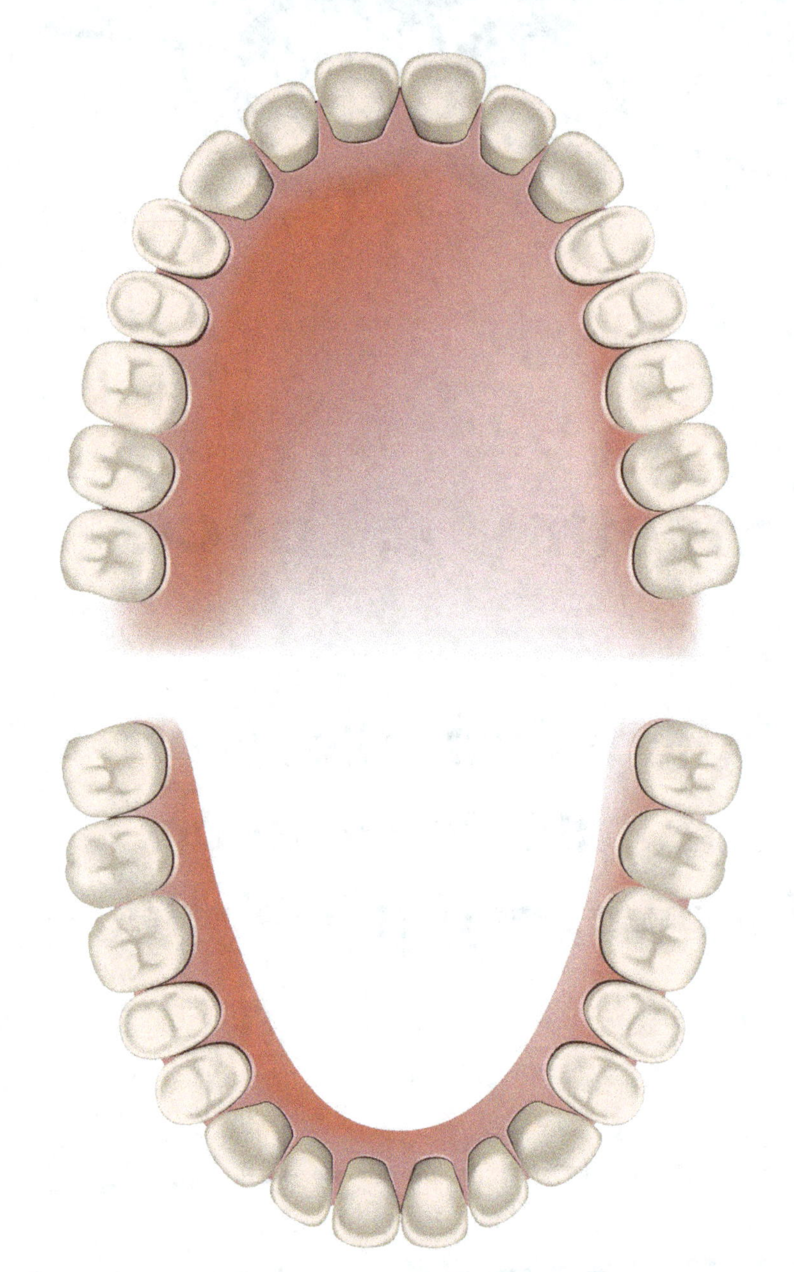

English
Spanish
tooth
diente
Teeth are like your bones, and are alive. They have their own blood supply, and nerves.

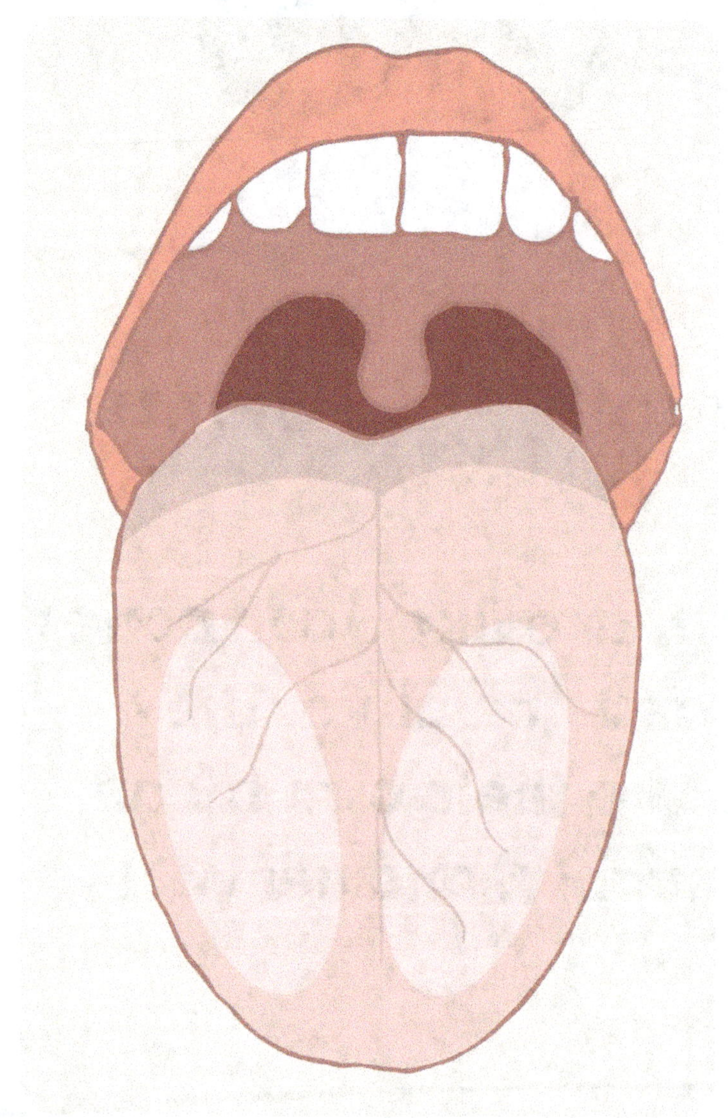

English
tongue
Spanish
lengua
Humans have unique
tongue prints, just like
we all have unique
fingerprints.

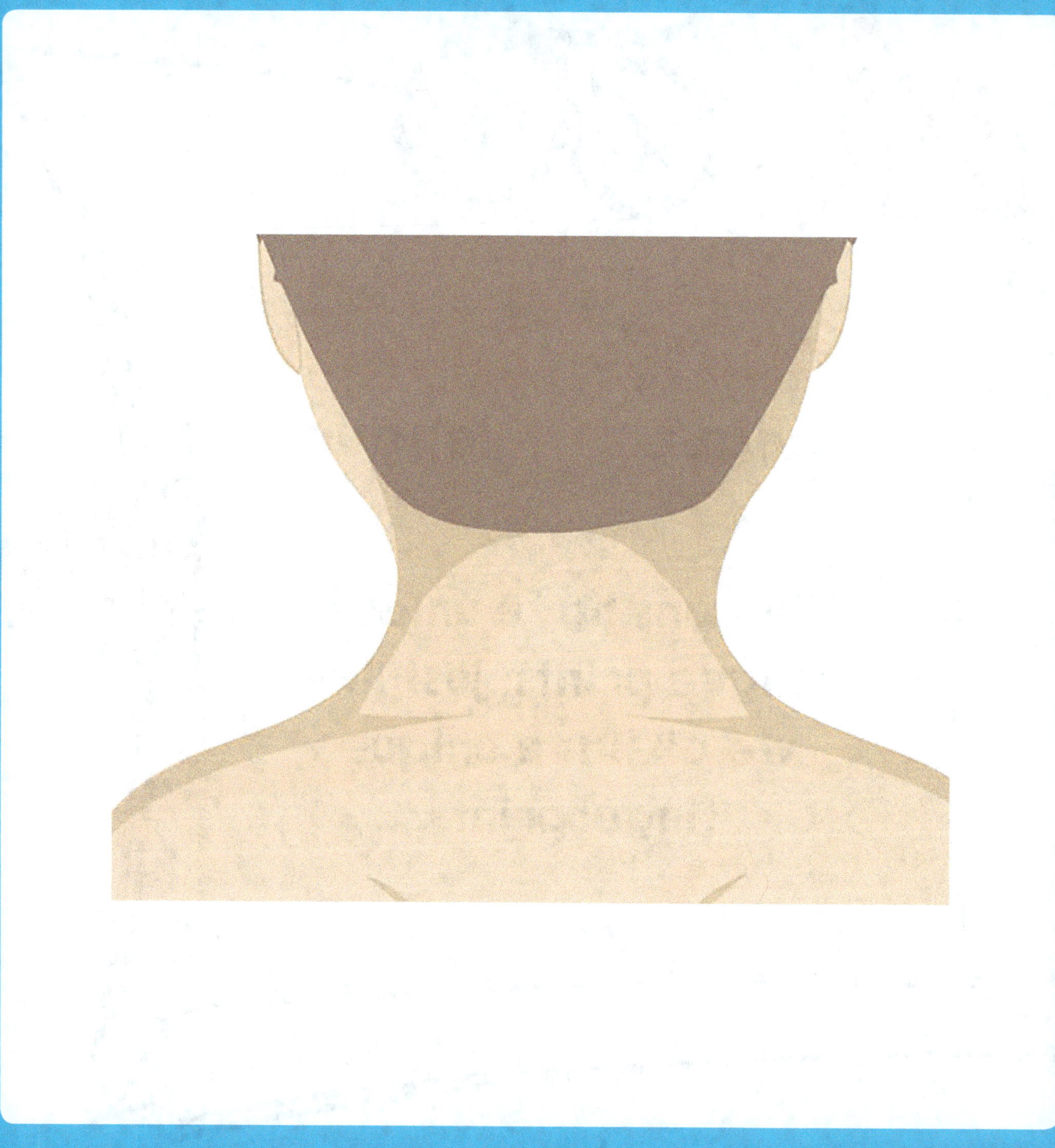

English
neck
Spanish
cuello
The human neck has the same number of vertebrae as a giraffe's neck.

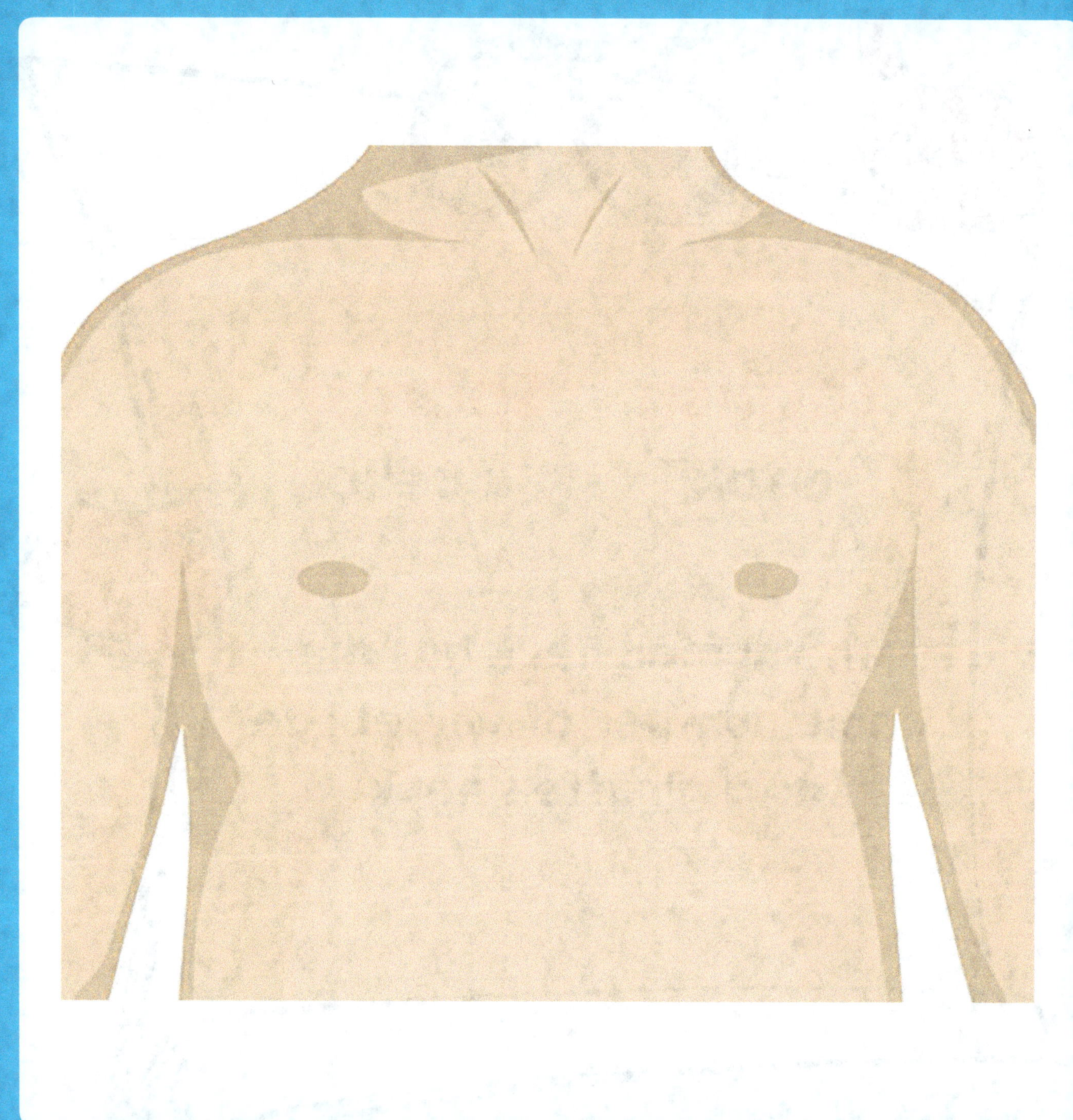

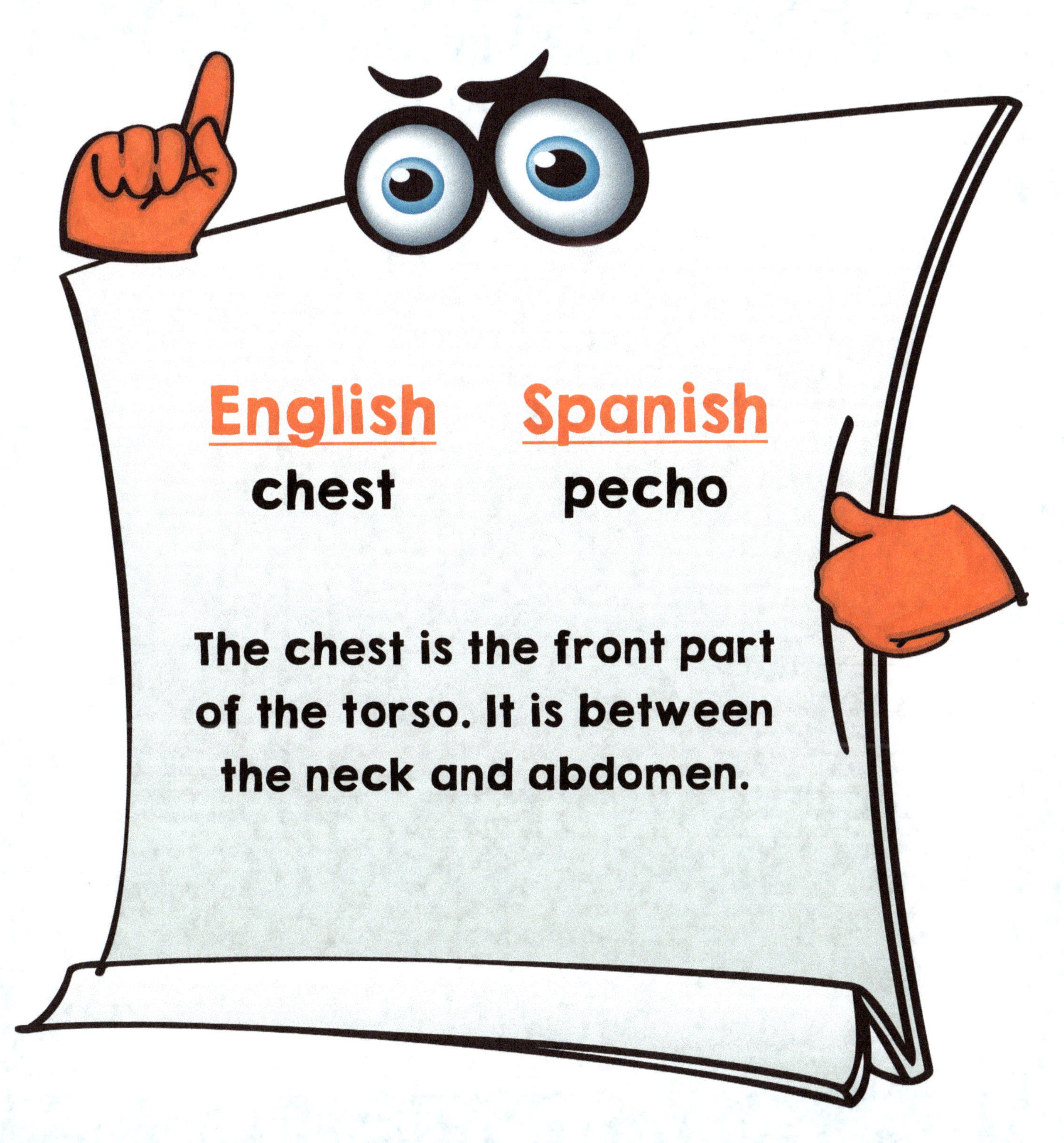

English
chest
Spanish
pecho
The chest is the front part of the torso. It is between the neck and abdomen.

English
Spanish
stomach
estómago
The stomach serves as a
first line of defense for
your immune system.

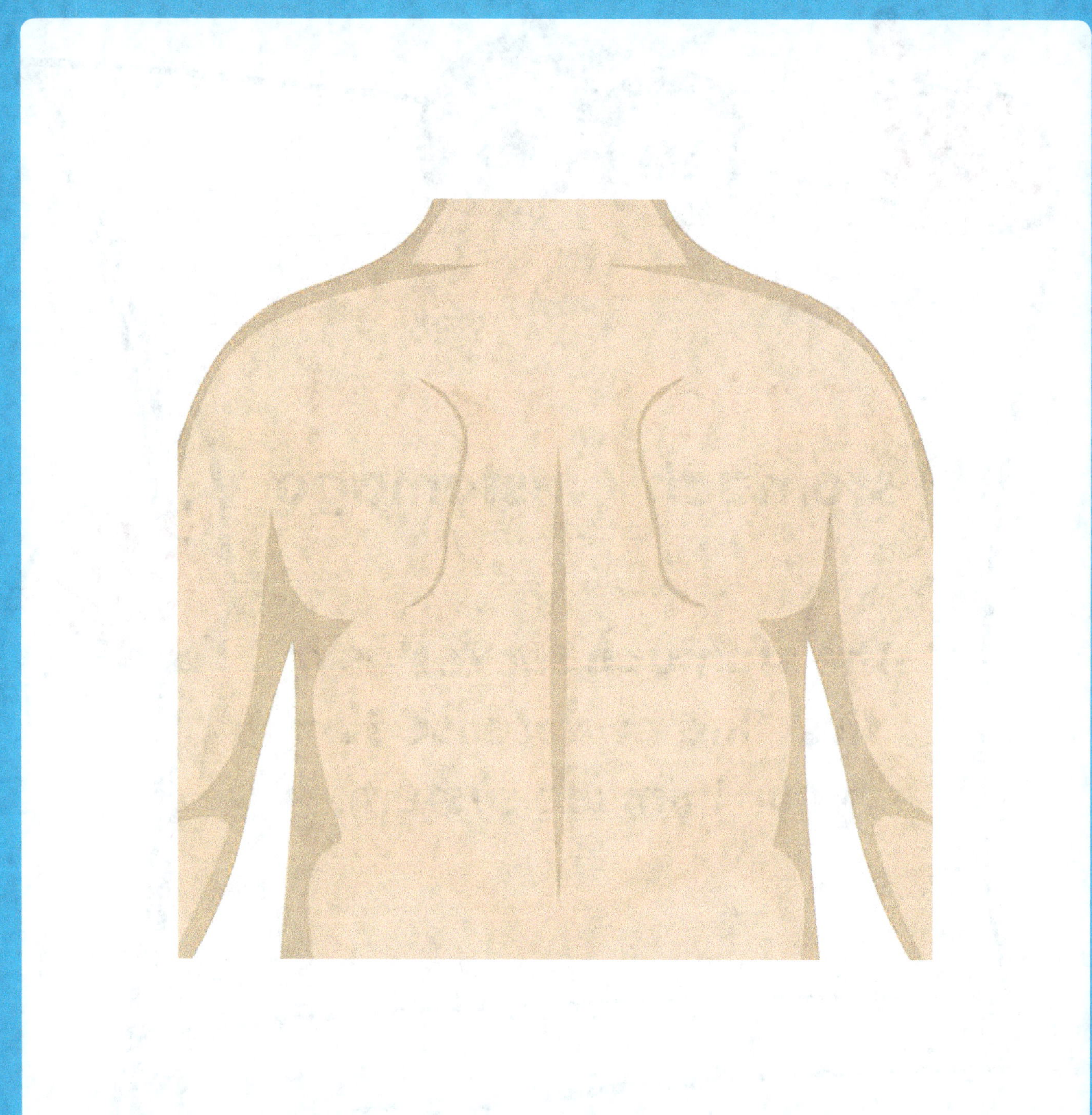

English
back

Spanish
espalda

The back is the surface
opposite to the chest.

English
arm
Spanish
brazo
The arm is made from three long bones, linked by a hinge joint at the elbow.

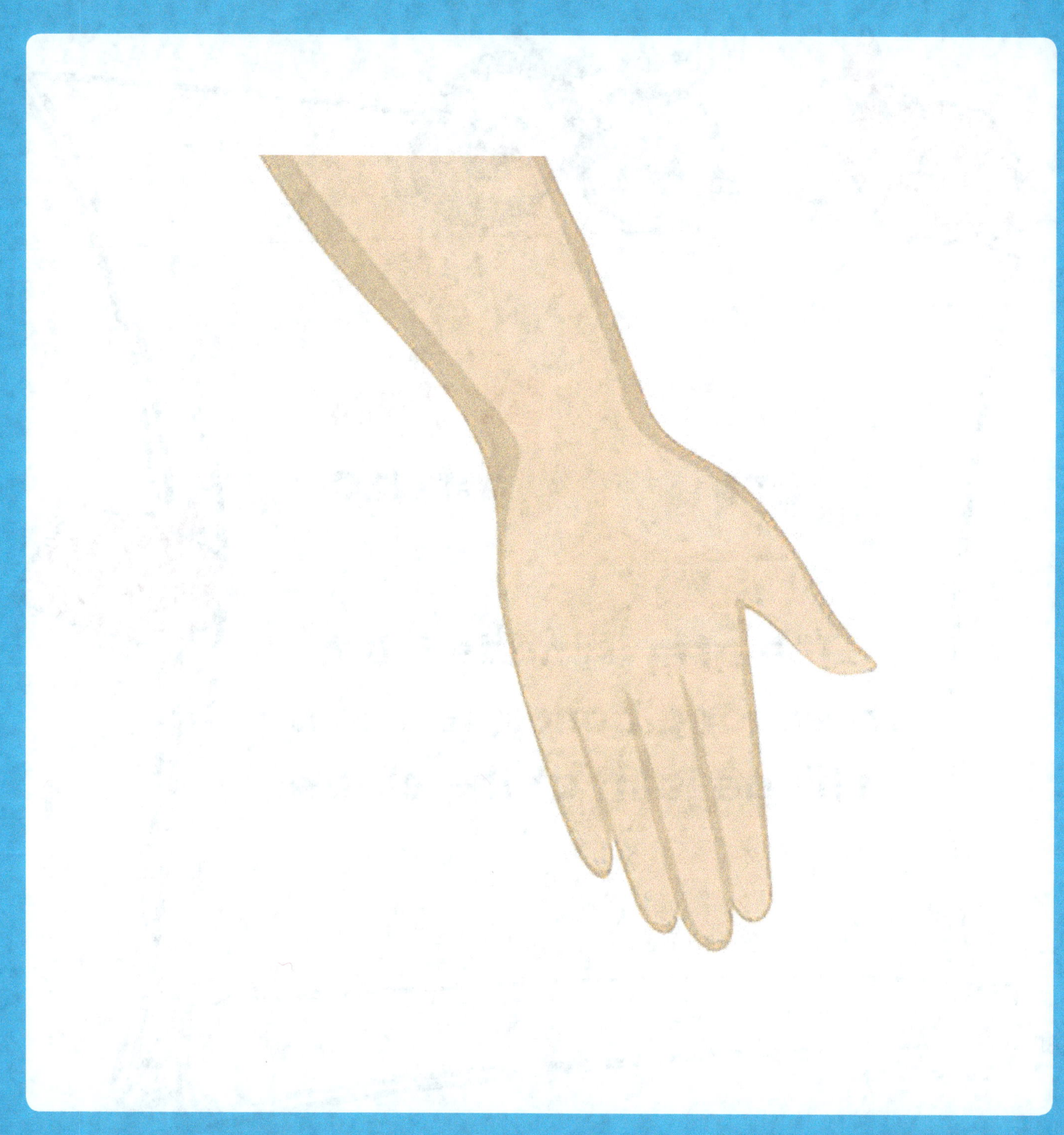

English
hand
Spanish
mano
The human hand has five fingers and 27 bones.

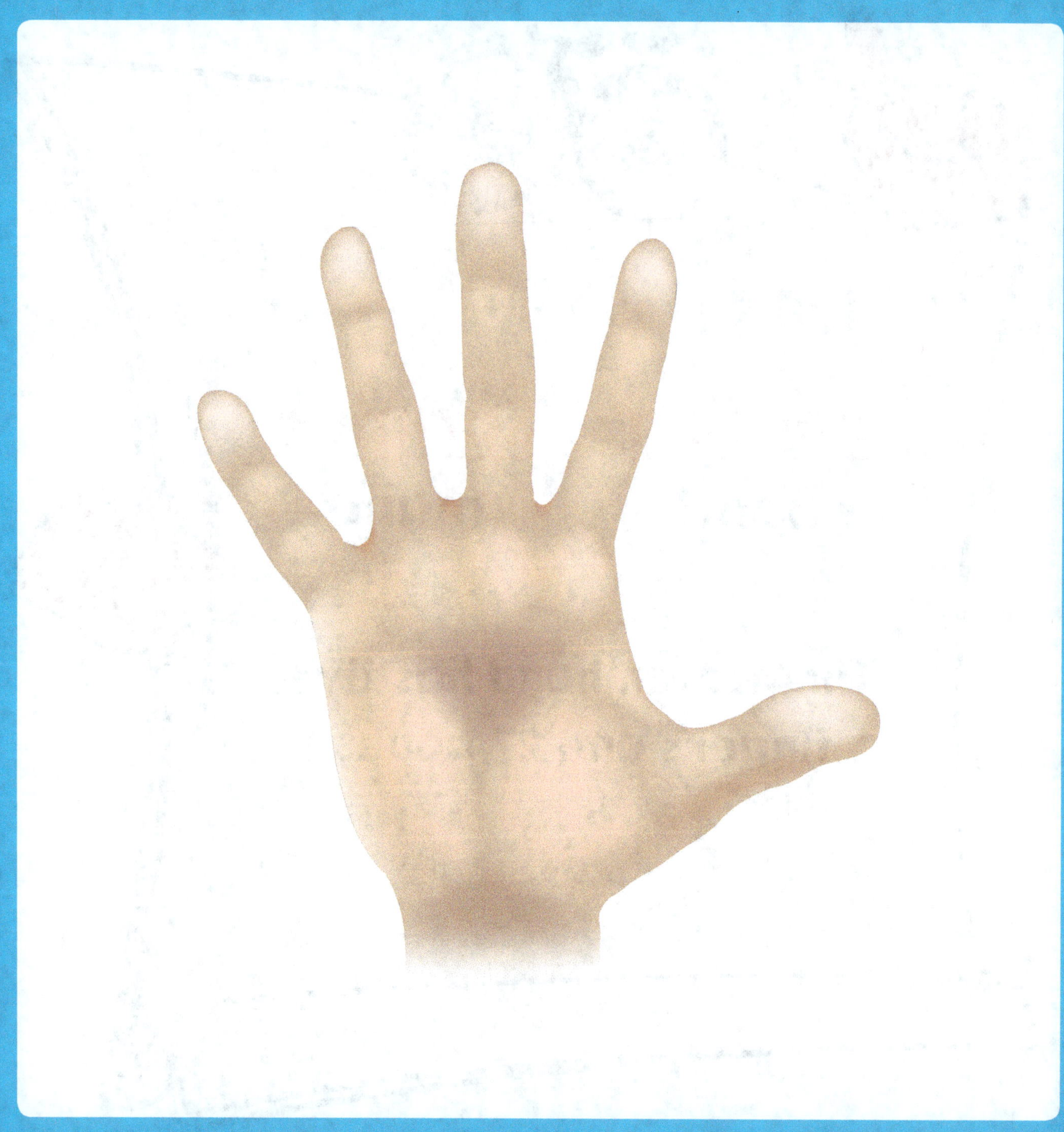

English
Spanish
finger
dedo
A finger is a type of digit attached to the hand. They are used for doing things and feeling things.

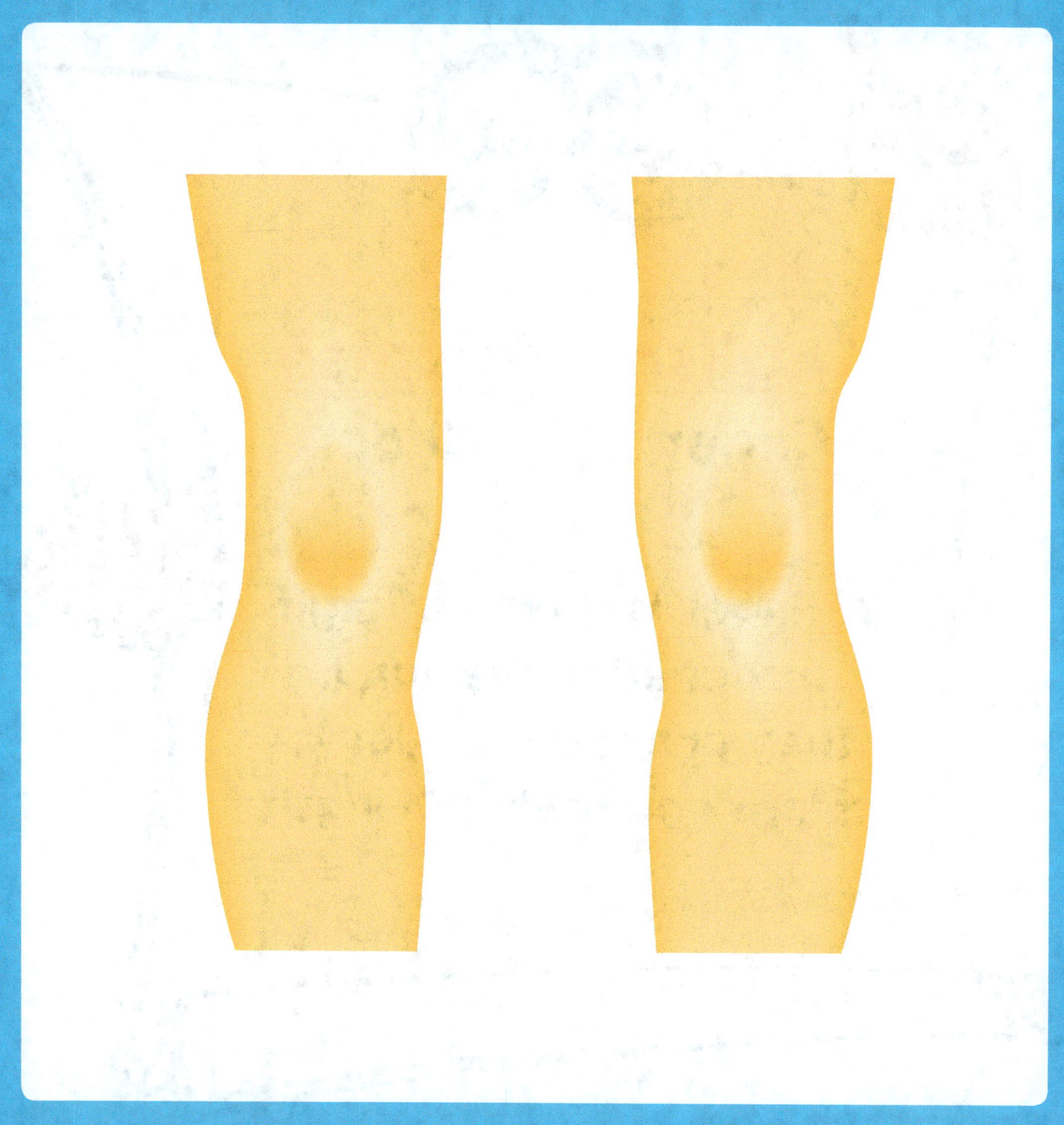

English
knee

Spanish
rodilla

The knee is the joint that links 4 of the upper and lower bones of the leg.

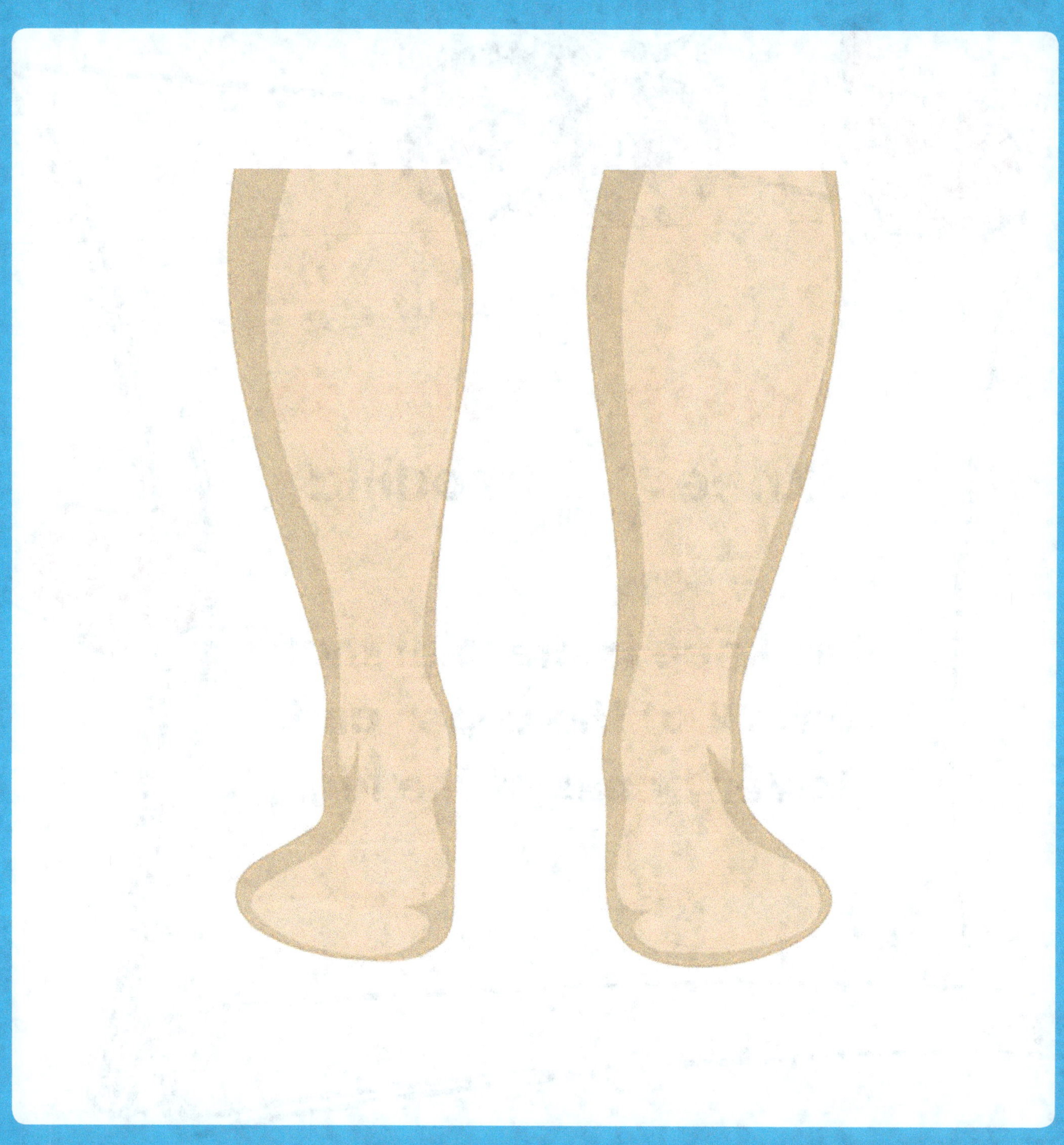

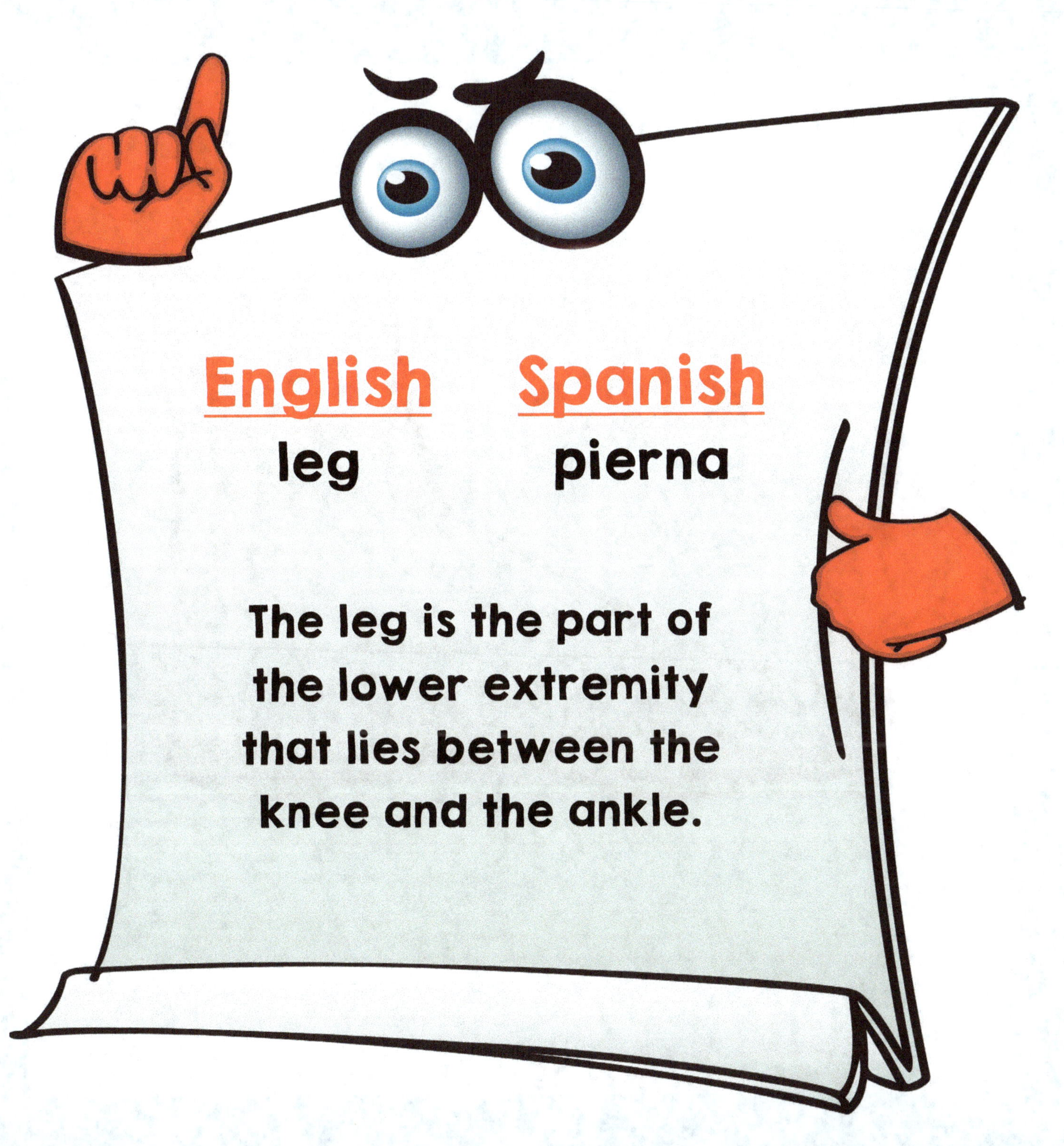

English
leg

Spanish
pierna

The leg is the part of the lower extremity that lies between the knee and the ankle.

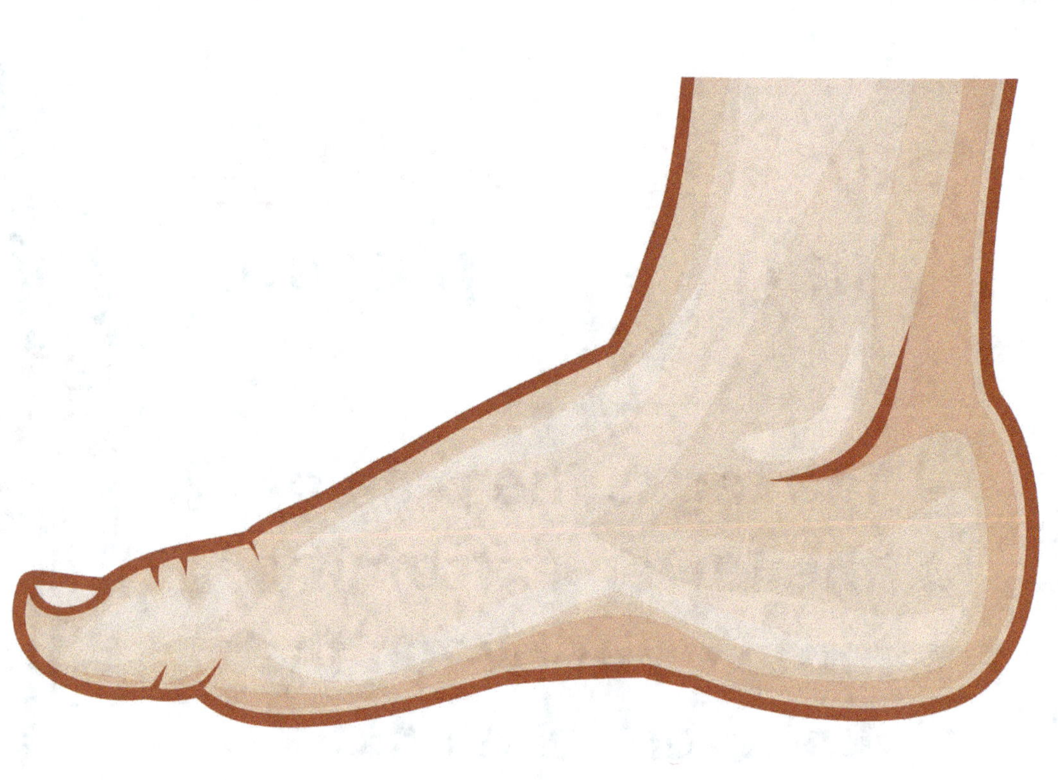

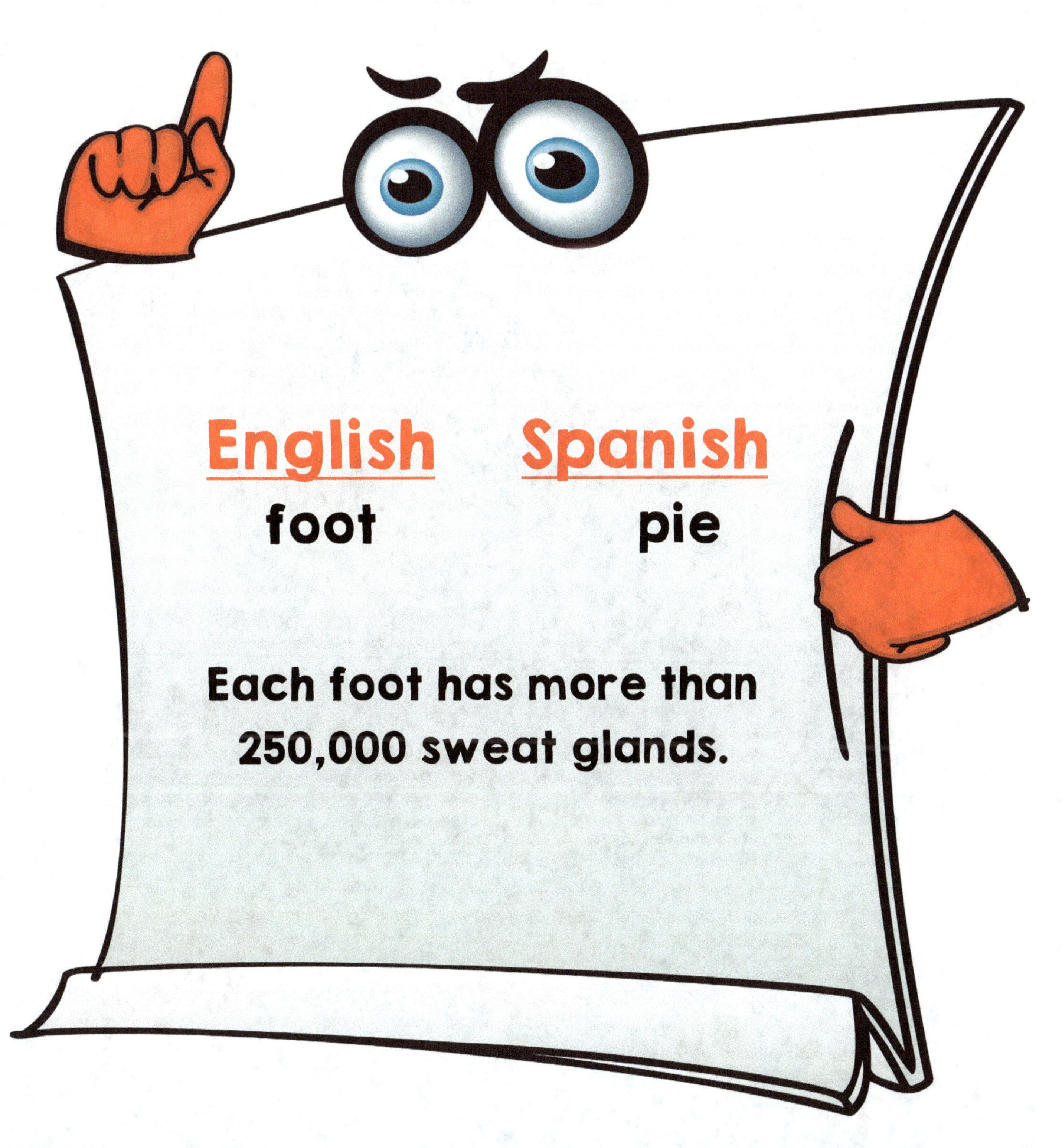

English
foot

Spanish
pie

Each foot has more than
250,000 sweat glands.

Visit

BABY PROFESSOR
EDUCATION KIDS

www.BabyProfessorBooks.com

to download Free Baby Professor eBooks
and view our catalog of new and exciting
Children's Books